Distaff

Jane Kite

for Briony and Leon

Published by Half Moon Books 2017,
an imprint of OWF Press Community Interest Company
Half Moon House, 9B Westgate, Otley, West Yorkshire LS21 3AT

www.owfpress.com

Cover illustration: Granger Historical Picture Archive/Alamy Stock Photo: Eve Spinning, c1350.
Eve spinning with a distaff, with two children in her lap and two in a cradle, which she rocks with her feet. Fresco, c1350, from the church at Kirkerup near Roskilde, Denmark.

Thanks to Rosalind Fairclough Proofreading Services

ISBN 978-0-9934275-9-6

Printed by
imprintdigital.com, Seychelles Farm, Upton Pyne, Devon EX5 5HY
info@imprintdigital.com

Acknowledgements

'Why did Auntie Alice keep falling over and breaking bones?' and 'Done' were previously published in separate editions of *The North* (Smith/Doorstop). 'Gap' appeared in *Chronicles of Eve* (Paper Swans Press, 2016). 'Honour' was awarded third prize in the *Segora* competition, 2015.

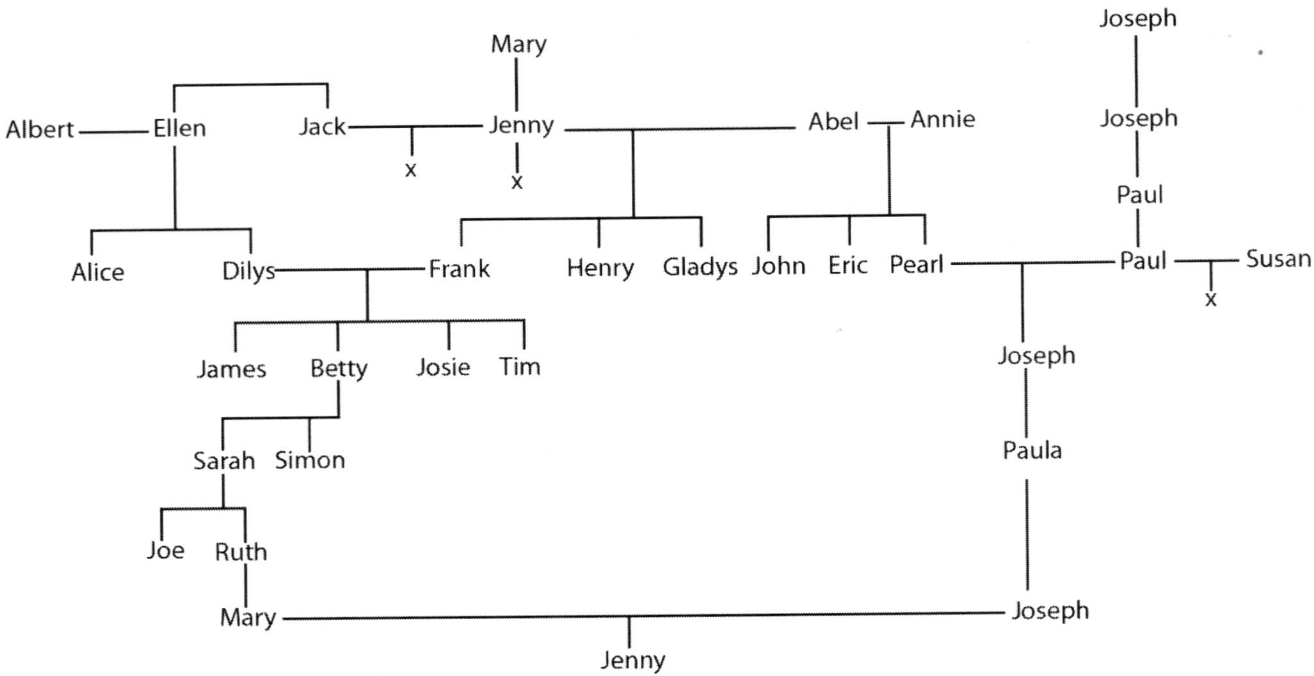
Joseph
Mary
Albert
Ellen
Jack
x
Jenny
x
Abel
Annie
Joseph
Paul
Alice
Dilys
Frank
Henry
Gladys
John
Eric
Pearl
Paul
Susan
x
James
Betty
Josie
Tim
Joseph
Sarah
Simon
Paula
Joe
Ruth
Mary
Joseph
Jenny

This collection of poems tells a story about an imagined family. It is a partial, untidy, disjointed and contradictory story of human frailty and a precarious joy in life. There are gaps to be tolerated or filled with something from your own imagining.

I would like to thank the poets who have helped in discussing drafts of these poems and also those who have helped me through their own writing and performance. In particular, thank you to all the Otley Poets and to Peter at Half Moon Books.

Contents

Cast of Characters

1887: Winter	Jenny, Joseph
1910: Abel and Jenny	Jenny, Abel, Henry, Frank, Gladys
1913: Across the Channel	Jenny, Jack
1916: Maison Tolérée	Jenny
1919: Enterprise	Jenny, Abel, Henry, Frank, Gladys
1929: Skipping song	Jenny
1941: Paying the rent	Dilys
1942: Land girl	Dilys
1948: Tomatoes	Dilys, James, Frank
1950: Annie singing	Annie
1953: Post-war	Betty, Frank
1954: Bathtime	Pearl, John
1955: Storm	Josie, Frank
1955: Spider	Josie
1956: Eggs	Josie, James
1956: Sister	Pearl, John, Eric
1956: Gathering	Alice, James, Betty, Josie, Tim
1957: Fires	James, Dilys
1957: Pearl	Pearl, Paula
1958: Paul 1	Paul, Susan
1958: Why did Auntie Alice keep falling over and breaking bones?	Betty, Alice
1959: Glad-eye	Betty, Gladys, Jenny
1961: Animals	James, Betty, Josie, Tim, Jenny
1962: Where has she gone?	Joseph, Pearl
1963: Cage	James
1965: Housework	Annie
1968: Cover	Annie

1972: Paul 2	Paul, Pearl
1972: Last house	Jenny
1980: Paul 3	Paul, Pearl, Joseph
1988: Return journey	James
1989: Bathing my old mother	James, Dilys
1990: Daffodils	Annie
1995: Gap	Simon
1995: Your hands	James, Dilys
1999: Near the end	Eric
2000: Honour	Dilys, Josie
2001: Dispossessed	Betty, James, Dilys, Frank, Jenny, Ellen, Albert, Abel
2004: Done	Betty, Frank
2006: Advice on dealing with nerves about public speaking	Betty, Sarah
2007: Being given the world	John
2009: Memoir	Josie
2010: Organised	Pearl
2014: Living with a cyborg	Betty, Ruth
2017: Boy upside down above trampoline	Tim, Joe
2018: Requiem	Tim
2020: Enough	Susan
2026: Warriors	Sarah, Mary
2045: Birth	Jenny, Joseph, Mary
new	Jenny

We are not all counted.
Some are born slippery,
make a quick getaway.

Some are slid through cracks
into tunnels and sewers
with no paperwork done.

Have you noticed
the ghouls sometimes
turn the other way?

If we are lucky, overlooked,
we might swim through the drains
to an open sea. After a pounding,

wash up somewhere
become marram grass,
root at the soft sand, latch on.

1887: Winter

She was dropped on a foul night into a running gutter
for death's welcome that would do for her by morning.
Except a man, walking with eyes downcast in grief,
saw the baby, plucked her up, tucked her,
naked and silent, into his own coat,
walked three miles to the convent door
and passed her in.

The sister asked for a name.
He mouthed the one on his mind –
his dead wife, Jenny.

Under the rule of woman, belt and crucifix,
she turned out a thriver, learnt to scorn weakness.
She was sweet-faced, nimble-fingered and obedient
once the devils her mother's sins had left in her
were beaten out. On his weekly visit to hear confession,
the priest would abase himself for a girl of five or less,
a sacrifice. He favoured Jenny.

Afterwards, the nuns would scourge the girl
in case she should believe herself desired.

The child kept close within the convent walls.
She did not like fresh air, feared storms and rain,
so made herself of use inside to all.
By nine she was adept at mending torn habits
and could make adjustments to the robes of priests,
could stitch and darn, tend a bitch at whelp,
scrub and scour and sluice and help to save
the nuns from giving birth to bastards.

When at twelve she bled, they heaped on
blessings and holy water. Gave her to the world.

1910: Abel and Jenny

For all his weskit, watch and Albert,
for all her pretty painted face,
they were no better than they ought to be.
Lived over the shop with their two bastard boys,
his true wife being confined ten years
behind asylum walls.

They each kept shop. Both could count,
he could write and read. On the corner
under three brass balls, he sold,
as well as gold and silver jewellery,
workers' shirts, clogs, overalls, flat caps,
trousers, linoleum, doormats,
and what was kept as forfeiture.

Those caught in a tight corner took
their pledges round the back: lockets,
signet rings, Sunday suits, blankets,
fiddles, button boots, all pushed across
the mahogany counter for pence or shillings
or a guinea and a ticket to keep
till they scraped enough to get them back,
else after a year and a week,
the unredeemed was lost.

The nuns had kept her till she was twelve
then sent her over the moors to earn her keep.
She skivvied hard, but had thoughts above her station
and as she fetched and carried about the town
she kept one eye on where her chance might come.

It was a brooch in Abel Duckworth's window.
She went in his shop to ask

if he might put the trinket aside
until she could pay. He saw a pretty face
and took her in to nurse his wife
and tend his offices.

In less than a year the wife was gone,
a boy was born and a second shop was had.

He patted his corporation, she grew bonny,
but their third-born was a sickly girl
and the mother, not wanting the tie,
cursed the child to death, but it didn't work.

By then he was knocking on sixty
and ailing with the droop,
so she took up with a fancy-man
and caught the steamer to France.
Left the old man sucking soup.

1913: Across the Channel

He was green-gilled on the boat
and spewed onto the fine red silk
of Jenny's stolen frock.
When they reached Le Havre,
where he quickly recovered,
the fancy-man scarpered
and Jenny sat on the harbour
in the stink of it and shivered.

But her blue eyes did their trick
and she found her way
with sailors and butchers
tailors and cobblers and tinkers.

And then the war was on.
She'd no fare back to England.
A gendarme picked her up
and dumped her at a Maison Tolérée.

1916: Maison Tolérée

Jenny watches from across the street,
in front of the basement where the girls sleep
along with a couple of the children they keep
hid away from the inspectors.

She watches from five o'clock
when the lads make their way past the dock
to queue on the steps, rattle the lock
of the Maison Tolérée.

At five to six she spits in the dirt,
gulps her pinard, gathers her skirts,
stubs the Gitanes, prepares for work
at the Maison Tolérée.

****

Six o'clock, the government says,
the red light's on,
we open our legs
for the fine British Tommies
all booted and putteed,
queued on the stairs,
larking about,
waiting for six o' clock.

These are the cocky ones
straight off the boat,
full of bravado,
full of spunk,
keen as mustard
to drop their keks
at the Maison Tolérée.

Next day at six,
the government says,
we open our legs to the boys
on leave from the front.
Still boys,
but shocked,
their eyes
wild fucking desperate
or dead.
They try to push through,
through their hell,
there's nothing else to do
at the Maison Tolérée.

And we are the girls
with our cock-eyed faces.
We are the girls with our
filthy flounces.
We are the girls with
the clap and the pox.
We are the girls,
our bodies insulted by
poor sod boys for a franc or two,
by government inspectors
with a job to do.

We do it, we get through,
what else is there to do
at the Maison Tolérée?

1919: Enterprise

She washed her face at the river,
smoothed her skirts as best she could,
begged a bun at the baker's to stave the pangs
and presented herself at the pledge office.
The old man lifted his eyes from the ledger,
saw the scrawny wretch that was Jenny,
caught his breath and felt his hoarded anger
dissipate. He lifted the counter and let her through.
They bargained. He said that Gladys, the sickly child,
was lame and upstairs and the boys had been sent away
for the sake of their education.

He took her behind the counter, but said she couldn't stay
as his needs as a rule were catered for now by Annie,
the butcher's daughter who he'd taken in
as housekeeper and to care for the girl.

But he couldn't bear to lose Jenny again,
so he unhooked a key from the wall
and handed it over, the key to the second shop.

Jenny slept for a couple of days in the upstairs room
then set to work with broom and bucket
putting the shop to rights.

And started it off as a milliner's
with a little of Madame's French flair –
hat blocks, dollies, needles, long pins,
ribbons, feather and fur.

Then she took to making a jugged hare lunch
on market day for the farmers and tinkers.
This grew into a full café, whilst in the back
where pigeons and rabbits hung on hooks,
she'd help out a woman in need for half a crown.

1929: Skipping song

Jenny in fox fur
Jenny in rabbit
Jenny in an overcoat
Jenny in a habit

Jenny chase the children
Jenny chase the men
Jenny poke your eye out
start again

1941: Paying the rent

The money's ready with the book
on the meter box by the front door.
He's late, so she might
get away with it
this time.

She's crouched at the foot
of the stairs, forehead pressed
against the rough cut edge
of the letterbox,
saying her prayers.

It's the right money,
one pound two and six,
so he won't have to fiddle
in his trouser pockets
for the change. Mrs S
at number 4 says
he tried it on with her,
and if he pushes in again
she'll slap his face.

These days every black market
shyster and wide-boy
chances his arm.
She could have fobbed him off
first time if she'd twigged,
didn't encouraged him,
not like Mrs S.

Footsteps come up
the path and stop.
She opens the door
as little as she can
get away with.

He picks up the money,
stuffs it in a shammy pouch,
uncaps a fountain pen,
fills in the book,
takes a mucky hanky out,
wipes his mouth.
Says, next week with a little bit of luck
he'll have time to come in,
have a cup of tea.

1942: Land girl

what I remember is

my hand on her warm womanly back
after we dispensed with the bolster

the delicious shock of her grimed
fingers in my knickers

her scamp eyes
her daring me

1948: Tomatoes

He sowed seeds, pricked out the young ones,
pinched away side shoots, tied thin limbs
to sticks on Sundays, when he was there.
The rest of the week was hers.
She watered at allotted times
between her duties to house and child,
mixed a solution of dried blood
to feed them, responded to his interrogation
on the telephone, checking on his darlings.
She watched them grow, and hated them.
When their time came, with the child
clutched to her skirt, her bony fingers
cradled the ripest, snapped them off,
put them in the box for the first day of the shop.
She admired their plumpness in spite of herself –
their firmness, the taut skin.
This was his harvest. The glut became her life;
the musty smell from the greenhouse
brought in with the box to the kitchen,
the weighing scales out of the cupboard,
paper bags strung on a cup hook, cash tin
ready and back door open for business.

Mostly by twos or fives in a bag,
each lot was put to the balance.
The child, grave-faced, tried to lift
a half-pound weight.

On Sunday, the man poked about
in the coins then tipped them
onto the kitchen table to count.

1950: Annie singing

She sang out of her head,
her mouth la-la-ing, the sound wandering
note after note, flowing moment on moment
without a thought of where it was coming
from or going, except for two songs
she knew word perfect:
There was an old woman who swallowed
a Fly and *On Ilkley Moor Baht 'at*.

She sang, verse on verse, with gusto
to their grisly ends.

1953: Post-war

We played on the crazy paving,
me and the red spider mites.
He pruned the Japanese honeysuckle
to within an inch of its life.

He taught the budgie to say its address
in case it ever got lost,
the dog to beg for kitchen scraps
and me to beg for him to stop.

1954: Bathtime

He's at the tap end,
legs akimbo.
I'm facing, in between,
trying not to let my feet
touch his thingy.

She's seen an advert
for bubble bath
in Woman's Own.
Pours in half a packet of Omo
then bats at our heads
with the carbolic.

1955: Storm

the button of his hellish macintosh
was pressed into her soft cheek
the wind lashed them together
and the rain and the sea spray beat
and her hair whipped at her face
and the rope bridge swayed
as it might upturn the world

she was held
she wished to be free
to belong to the sea

1955: Spider

Library books, they said, are notorious
carriers of infectious disease
and we don’t go to the cinema,
for fear of catching fleas.

Don’t be too clever or you will go mad.

We are not common and buy comics
or get our clothes from the tallyman.
You can have an ice cream
(but I don’t like ice cream) from the van.

Don’t be shy,
hold your money up high.
Say please. Say thank you.
Extra dragon’s blood?
But I don’t like ice-cream.

Lucky are: putting your clothes on inside out
(but not on purpose, and
not if you then change them round).
Dog with a good home
(she said: *next time I come on this earth I will be*
a dog with a good home).
New moon, when you turn your money over.

Little spider, little lucky money spider spidering
over my hand.
Don’t go out without money in your pocket.
Lucy Locket lost her pocket.

Don’t be too clever or you will go mad.

Unlucky are: cracked mirror, spilt salt (so throw some
over your left shoulder and into
the eye of the devil) and some children.

The wind coming down the chimney and putting out the fire
and the cold kitchen and her always-wet hands and the blood
running
with the water from the gushing tap when she held her cut
finger under it
and my pet rabbit who I called Lucky but who wasn't because I
starved him to death

and fools and children who shouldn't see things till they're
done.

Don't be too clever or you will go mad.

1956: Eggs

Her brother's stolen eggs
rested on cotton wool,
each in its own hollow
in the dark wood box.
Eggs from tits and warblers, finches,
raptors, owls and garden birds,
lines of eggs in their different guises,
dappled, brown blotched and speckled,
translucent blue, white, eau de nil,
some with a slight sheen, some chalky,
each one perfect, but for a pair of pin pricks
through which the life had been blown out,
leaving these skulls.

1956: Sister

She scrubs the tide mark off his neck
and puts him with sparse love
between starched sheets,
folded down and tucked so tight
he cannot wriggle free.

She sides the dishes,
clips her hair up,
paints her lips,
looks at bits of herself
in the compact mirror,
tells him to be good.

1956: Gathering

She stands at the gate and whistles for Jip –
counts like waiting for thunder
till she hears the muffled thid-thud of him running
before he rounds the bend, full speed, keen-eyed
to see she's pleased. She pats him and points to the lights
she's boiled and chopped and put in the yard.

She sings out the names of the children –
Betty, Jamie, and Josie. She casts a quick eye
over each to check for hurts. Nods them
into the kitchen to get their tea,
leans on the gate with her back to the house.
There's a boy at the open window shouts:
Auntie Alice, are you coming in?

1957: Fires

She was a bit of a witch.
If the fire threatened to die
she'd sprinkle sugar on it,
muttering incantations
to the god of sweetness,
prop the shovel in the grate,
then put up a sheet of newspaper
to draw and tell me to see it didn't catch.

This usually did the trick. The draught
would suck at the paper and I could watch
a spot turn brown, spread and darken.
Sometimes a red-edged hell-hole formed,
then hey presto! pull the paper off
like a magician with a tablecloth.

She fried chips in the big blackened
pan of fat. Every now and again it set on fire.
We knew what to do. Get my school blazer off the hook,
wrap it round your hands, grab the pan handle,
walk backwards slowly through the back door
and tip the whole flaming mess onto the earth.

1957: Pearl

She's pregnant.
How I wish I could be pleased.
I am knitting a matinee jacket.
She will not cope.
I fear for the child.
My oversight will not be enough.
I have dropped a stitch.

1958: Paul 1

We were sixteen.
He gets born. He's mine.
The sight of him cracks me open.

She gave it away.

1961: Animals

Grandma's best hat was trimmed with Astrakhan,
the pelt of a foetus lamb. Glass fox eyes watched
from the camphored stole she shouldered.

Sawdust on the butcher's floor
for soaking in the blood,
hooks for the hollowed carcasses
and a split, scrubbed, yellowed block.
I was sent for belly or scrag or chops
and watched the cleaver. On the bench,
kidney fat was peeled to reveal
a blushing blueness, nearly alive,
and the bloody liver of lambs lay down
as the knife sliced.

Grandma could cook a good jugged hare,
the gravy was rich and thick.
She'd hang the hare three weeks in the shed
to fatten the maggots, that was her trick.

We made marionettes
of a chicken's chopped-off feet
and chased the girls with them.
Auntie wore a rabbit's foot for luck.
She showed me the four new
flat-eared kittens, took them to the butt
just before dinner.

Grandma sat down and belched.
Took the parson's nose for herself.

1962: Where has she gone?

they said she was in The Slough of Despond
or was it like the butcher's peroxide wife
Prestwich the loony bin
taken in a yellow van

Mrs H who'd lost her son
accosted me coming back from the shops
and I shouldn't have carried
her two tins of cat food down to her house
and gone in and stayed until she stopped
talking and forgot I was there

I went home
he was beating the dog
she was baking buns

you only remember the picture
before the moment
before it happens

and afterwards
she was in the Slough of Despond
which is a bit mixed up in my mind
with the Trough of Bowland
a beautiful place so no connection
except the lurch in the stomach
when you're taken in the car

1963: Cage

Cuttlefish bone in the budgie’s cage,
pumice stone in the bathroom,
that cold place.

Cuttlefish bone
for the caged bird to peck,
pumice to hone your segs.

You covered the cage at night,
a cloth of white,
and then a cloth of black.

Pumice stone
to plane it away.

1965: Housework

I empty the old water
and fill the crystal vase afresh
for last week's flowers –
they have a day or so left.
There's a sad story
on the wireless
– a child who fell
down a disused well.

I dust the banister and skirting boards,
remove yesterday's Evening News
from the table, glance at the headline
about a small body found on the moors.

There's a stain on the kitchen window.
My neighbour's outside with her boy.
The girl was a trouble and had to be put away.

I wipe over the mantlepiece ornaments,
the blown-glass swan, the china dog and its pup.
I am safe from all that, with my lack.
Each month's jolt is the wrench of a thing
that will not happen.

I straighten up the maps my husband
has left out, dust the globe, rock his world
slow on its axis. My earth is flat
and has precipitous edges.

I fetch the Hoover from under the stairs,
watch its brown bag inflate, push
the monster that I hate
around the lounge to suck up imagined dirt.

I still have my bedroom slippers on,
and think of the ones my mother wore,
blue checked felt with pompoms.
Sometimes I inhabit her old body
and my tread is tentative.
I take the stairs with care,
remembering her fall.
Something pierced her heart.
There is a glass tine in me,
a sharp quill.

1968: Cover

Sometimes with you
I have to wear a flak
jacket and hard hat
to prevent mortal damage
or a cracked mind.
But in the squall
of this quarrel
I want to wrap
us in a soft blanket
away from the wind.

1972: Paul 2

I believe it is a woman's right to choose.
She lets go my hand, walks towards
the glass doors of the clinic.

The crack in me hurts.

1972: Last house

For half a century she bought and sold
to make a steady increase in her stock
of property. With guile, she plied her trades,
could ride the market, take the ups and downs.
She thrived, she starved, lured men, bore children,
loved and was abandoned, ran into trouble
and out again. Was feared. And then,

with creeping age and crippling hands,
she lost her grip. Fortune reversed.
Matters went from bad to worse.

This house, small and dark, huddles to the church.
Inside, an ebony dresser takes up half the room.
In these confines, in the gloom of forty watts,
the death-bed tapestry she lived with easily
for twenty years now preys on her mind.
A budgerigar with only one eye looks on.

At night she covers its cage with a sewn
cloth of white, and then a cloth of black,
like she is robing a religious.

She has cut and stitched a slit for the wire handle.
For the bird, a chink of light.

What the bird finds is her mouth
wanting to kiss him goodnight.
A bird does not want to kiss.

The bird is gasping for air and light.

1980: Paul 3

I brought my wife to the hospital.
Her waters broke at home.
It is like dread, this waiting.
I'll go to the pub after.
Not show I'm broken.

1988: Return journey

On the train, for the back rhythm
and eating up the miles
I put between us to go
looking for an edge
to balance on.
Edges have their own line in
security and I kept my eyes
fixed forward as I wept.

As a child, rocking on two legs
of a rickety stool
in front of the open fire
where my mother used to toast
the insides of her thighs,
they said I was hell-bent
and would burn,
but I never fell.

So I have had my
arms outstretched
to judge my weight
and test the pace
for coming back.

1989: Bathing my old mother

You are the little one you have always been –
your curled and discoloured body
like a beaten child, your wrinkled dugs
hanging pitiful,
your tilted head – a question?
No, just a trick, distorting your old body.

But was there, was there,
a vital light in your eye –
to remind me of the old terror?

1990: Daffodils

Cut down, laid low, banded in bundles,
packed layer on layer in a box,
they sealed up their stems for an arid flight.
Now, like yarrow sticks ready to divine
or little spears to pierce the year to life,
they're dunked in a bucket by the market man.

I choose my lot of ten completely closed,
buds not yet even plumped.
Carry them, resting in my elbow crook,
home to the kitchen, cut the elastic,
trim their stalk ends one by one and stand them
in a glass. I wait for their yellow to fill a vacancy.

1995: Gap

I watch in admiration as a barefoot
novice nun mops the expanse
of the orphanage floor, pushes
a wet cloth over the tiles with her feet
like they are hands, uses her toes
to niggle into corners.

Traditional ways attract me, but the priest
wants me to know how modern they are
and how grateful to the mother church
that donates the yellow fluid they use
to keep the institution clean.
I smile at him and then at her.

She lifts a foot, holds it upturned in her hand
to show me the sole, fissured and raw.

1995: Your hands

Not gloved, no rings,
stiff and tremulous now,
skin thinned and creped,
knuckles thickened.

They have pushed and shoved,
carried and skinned,
slopped, mopped blood and spit,
have polished to a high shine,
did not stop their splitting,
their chopping and knitting together
while it was necessary to go on.

They beckoned my father,
held him, waved him away,
bore his return, cupped my baby head,
slapped my child legs.

Your hands dirtied and washed,
held on tight, braced against the odds.
Let go. Wrung out.

1999: Near the end

You see me calloused; I am raw inside.
Breath rasps through burnt pipes. I shuffle,
eyes down, still looking for a butt-end to chew
from habit, but I can't reach them now.

I turn a discarded sandwich with my shoe
like a dead body and its innards spew pink
and green on the pavement. I spit acid.
Will you sweep me up?

2000: Honour

I am eating yogurt with a plastic knife
in honour of the woman who,
if only there had been some logical thread
in the stream of her consciousness, well
it might have been better for both of us.

She lived on chocolate. For my fortieth she came
on the first bus at five thirty a.m. to pop Milk Tray in
with a note – *H Birthday, know you don't*
like chocolate but it fits through the letterbox.

She lacked something to check the chaos, and he,
bad man, all shiny shoes and Windsor knot,
would put the fear of God into her,
not that she was religious, but she knew
how to be afraid and in a crisis
would squeeze her eyes tight shut, clam up her ears
and stay like that until it was over,
whatever it was that she never saw,
never heard, never saw him, bad man
with clean hands and the rest of him stinking.

For the slattern that he said she was,
I hold up this plastic knife, licked clean.